鳥 山 明

One nice thing about being a manga artist is that you can pick your own days off. For example, when you go to an *onsen* (hot springs) or Disneyland, you can avoid the week-ends when it's really crowded. You just have to go when the weather's good. You can even just drop everything and decide to go on a trip tomorrow! And on weekdays, the hotels have lots of vacancies. But now all of a sudden, my son is in elementary school, so I can't do that stuff anymore. There's traffic on the streets, the trains are crowded...agggh!

–Akira Toriyama, 1993

Widely known all over the world for his playful, innovative storytelling and humorous, distinctive art style, **Dragon Ball** creator Akira Toriyama is also known in his native Japan for the wildly popular **Dr. Slump**, his previous manga series about the adventures of a mad scientist and his android "daughter." His hit series **Dragon Ball** ran from 1984 to 1995 in Shueisha's **Weekly Shonen Jump** magazine. He is also known for his design work on video games such as **Dragon Warrior**, **Chrono Trigger** and **Tobal No. 1**. His recent manga works include **Cowa!**, **Kajika**, **Sand Land**, **Neko Majin**, and a children's book, **Toccio the Angel**. He lives with his family in Japan.

DRAGON BALL Z VOL.18
The SHONEN JUMP Manga Edition

This graphic novel contains material that was originally published in English in **SHONEN JUMP** #22-24.

STORY AND ART BY
AKIRA TORIYAMA

English Adaptation/Gerard Jones
Translation/Lillian Olsen
Touch-up Art & Lettering/Wayne Truman
Design/Sean Lee
Editor/Jason Thompson

Editor in Chief, Books/Alvin Lu
Editor in Chief, Magazines/Marc Weidenbaum
VP of Publishing Licensing/Rika Inouye
VP of Sales/Gonzalo Ferreyra
Sr. VP of Marketing/Liza Coppola
Publisher/Hyoe Narita

In the original Japanese edition, DRAGON BALL and DRAGON BALL Z are known collectively as the 42-volume series DRAGON BALL. The English DRAGON BALL Z was originally volumes 17-42 of the Japanese DRAGON BALL.

Printed in the U.S.A.

Published by VIZ Media, LLC
P.O. Box 77010
San Francisco, CA 94107

SHONEN JUMP Manga Edition
10 9 8 7 6 5 4
First printing, December 2004
Fourth printing, August 2007

SHONEN JUMP GRAPHIC NOVEL

DRAGON BALL Z

Vol. 18

DB: 34 of 42

STORY AND ART BY
AKIRA TORIYAMA

THE MAIN CHARACTERS

CELL
An artificial life form created by the late Dr. Gero. It absorbed Androids #17 and #18.
ANDROID #16
Although he was originally created to destroy Son Goku, Android #16 seems to be a good guy.
TRUNKS
The future son of Vegeta and Bulma, he is a half-human, half-Saiyan.
VEGETA
The prince of the Saiyans. He has trained long and hard for the battle with Cell.
Son Goku was Earth's greatest hero, and the Dragon Balls—which can grant any wish—were Earth's greatest treasure. Three years ago, Earth was visited by Trunks, a time traveler from the future, who warned of a coming attack by super-powerful androids. But even the androids didn't know that they were only the advance guard for an even more terrifying enemy: Cell, a bioweapon who absorbed the hapless androids and mutated into the ultimate fighter! Cell challenged the world to the "Cell Game" fighting tournament, promising to kill every human being if Earth could not bring forth a fighter who could defeat it. Unaware of the existence of the super warriors, the rest of humanity sent a champion, Hercule, who insisted on fighting Cell first. Now, while Hercule licks his injured pride, the real fight begins...

DRAGON BALL Z 18

ドラゴンボール

DRAGON BALL

DBZ:203
Cell vs. Son Goku

READ THIS WAY

IT'S... ABOUT TO BEGIN...
YEAH...
SHOW ME WHAT YOU CAN DO... KAKARROT.

ZSH

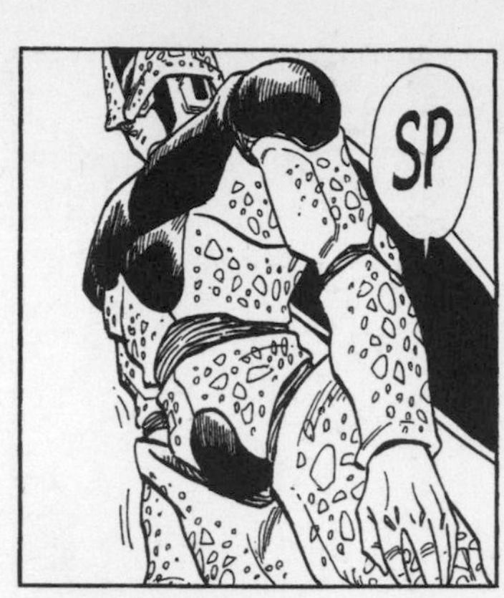
SP

GRIP

SO YOU'RE GOING TO START US OFF, EH?
I'D WANTED TO SAVE THE BEST FOR LAST... OH WELL.

READ
THIS
WAY

ZIP

NOW WE'LL FINALLY GET AN ANSWER... **WHY** WAS GOKU SO CALM?

...

D-DON'T WORRY, PEOPLE OF EARTH!! HERCULE SLIPPED AND FELL OUT OF BOUNDS, BUT HE'LL FIGHT CELL AGAIN AFTER A SHORT BREAK!!

READ THIS WAY

AND DURING THAT BREAK, ONE OF THOSE **FOOLS** WHO REFUSES TO LISTEN TO OUR WARNINGS WILL SHOW US HOW HE THINKS HE CAN FIGHT!

WELL, LET HIM LEARN HIS LESSON! SOME STUPIDITY ONLY DEATH CAN CURE!
HERCULE, WHAT DO **YOU** THINK OF THIS UNKNOWN CONTESTANT?
ZT

HEH HEH HEH... I CAN TELL JUST BY LOOKING AT HIS BUILD AND STANCE THAT HE'S AN AMATEUR.
HE WOULDN'T LAST TWO SECONDS AGAINST ME. I'LL GIVE HIM FIVE AGAINST CELL!

HA HA!
I GUESS THIS WON'T BE MUCH OF A BREAK FOR ME—BUT IT'LL BE ENTERTAINING!
LET'S GO!

WOG

SHP

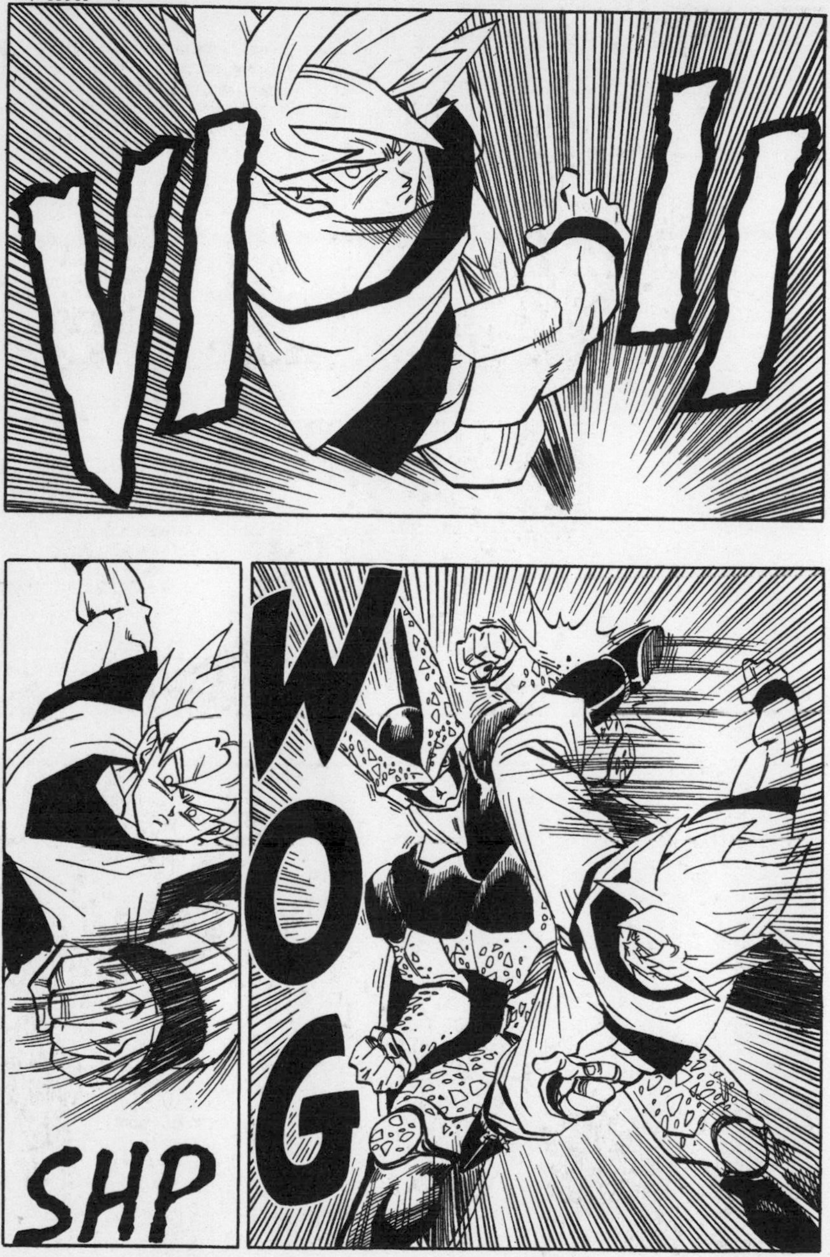

BIP
BAP
GOOM

READ THIS WAY

VM VM VM VM
VIII

FSH

VMMM

THOG

SCRRR

READ THIS WAY

BAMM

READ THIS WAY

READ THIS WAY

VNN

KHOOON

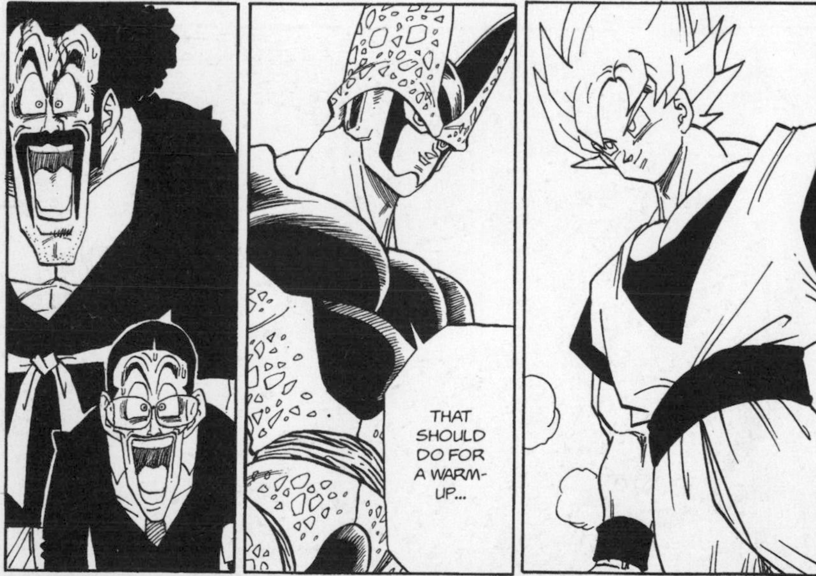

NEXT: Goku Opens It Up

DBZ:204 • Full Power

READ THIS WAY

N-NOW THE REAL FIGHT'S GONNA START...

DID I SEE HIM ACTUALLY PULLING OFF SOME GOOD MOVES...?
WH- WHAT DO YOU SAY, HERCULE...?

HUH?!

OH!
HE...UH... HE'S A LITTLE BETTER THAN I THOUGHT, YEAH!
BUT HE MUST BE REALLY PUSHING HIS LIMITS!

SON GOKU... IS A SEASONED WARRIOR, INDEED. THERE'S NO COMPARISON BETWEEN HIM AND THE OTHERS.

CELL'S TOUGHER THAN I EXPECTED... I'LL BE QUICK-FRIED IF I LET UP FOR A SECOND...

READ THIS WAY

ALL RIGHT !!
HSST

THAT LOOK IN GOKU'S EYES... !

THIS WILL BE FULL POWER.

WOOM

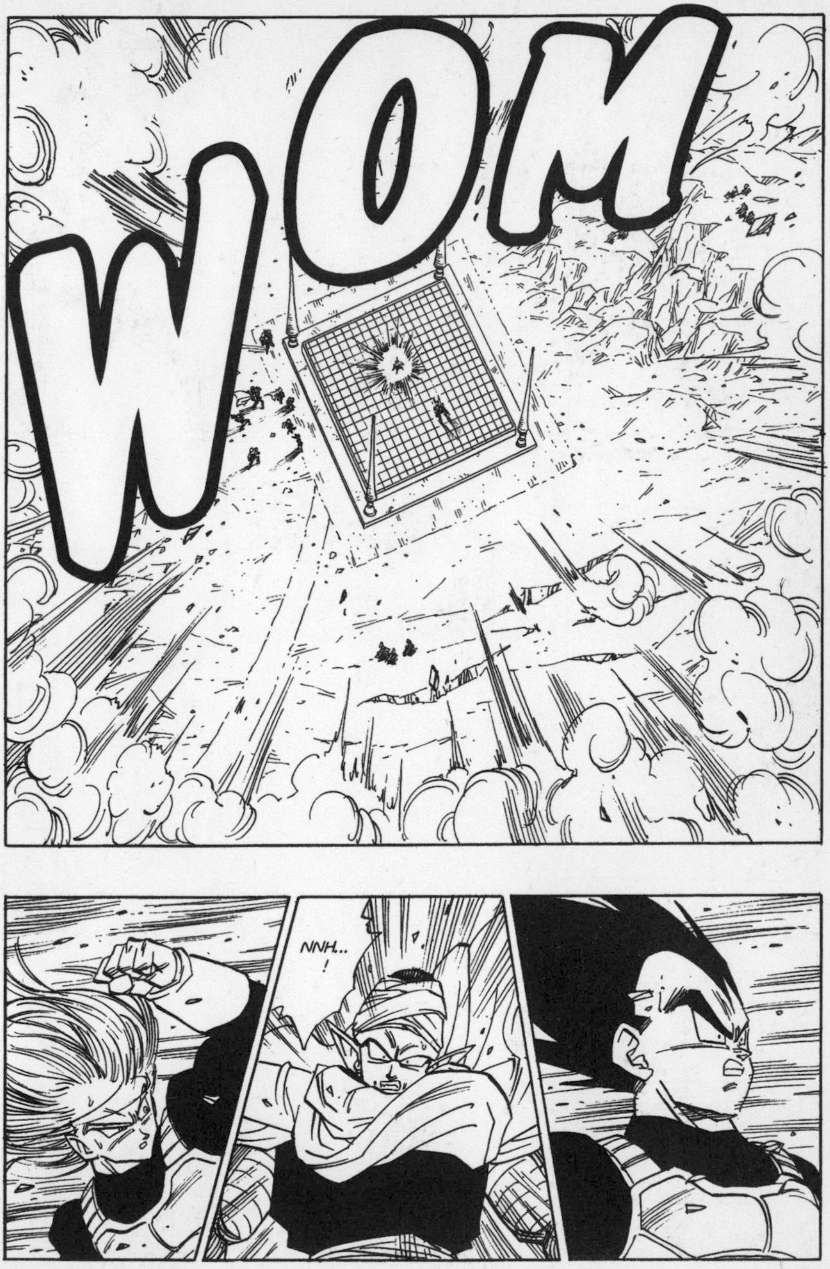

WOM

READ THIS WAY

HSSS...

READ THIS WAY

H-HIS CHI IS IMMEASURABLE...! HE'S B-BEYOND ALL OF US!

...

...WHY IS EVERYONE SO AMAZED...?
OF COURSE DAD'S GREAT... BUT...

WH- WH-WHAT JUST HAPPENED...?
IT FELT LIKE AN EXPLOSION... AND NOW THE UNKNOWN CONTESTANT SEEMS TO BE EMITTING FLAMES...

HEH..

HYAH
!!!
BO OM

WOOSH

ZZT ZZT

YEEP
!

UNH...
!!

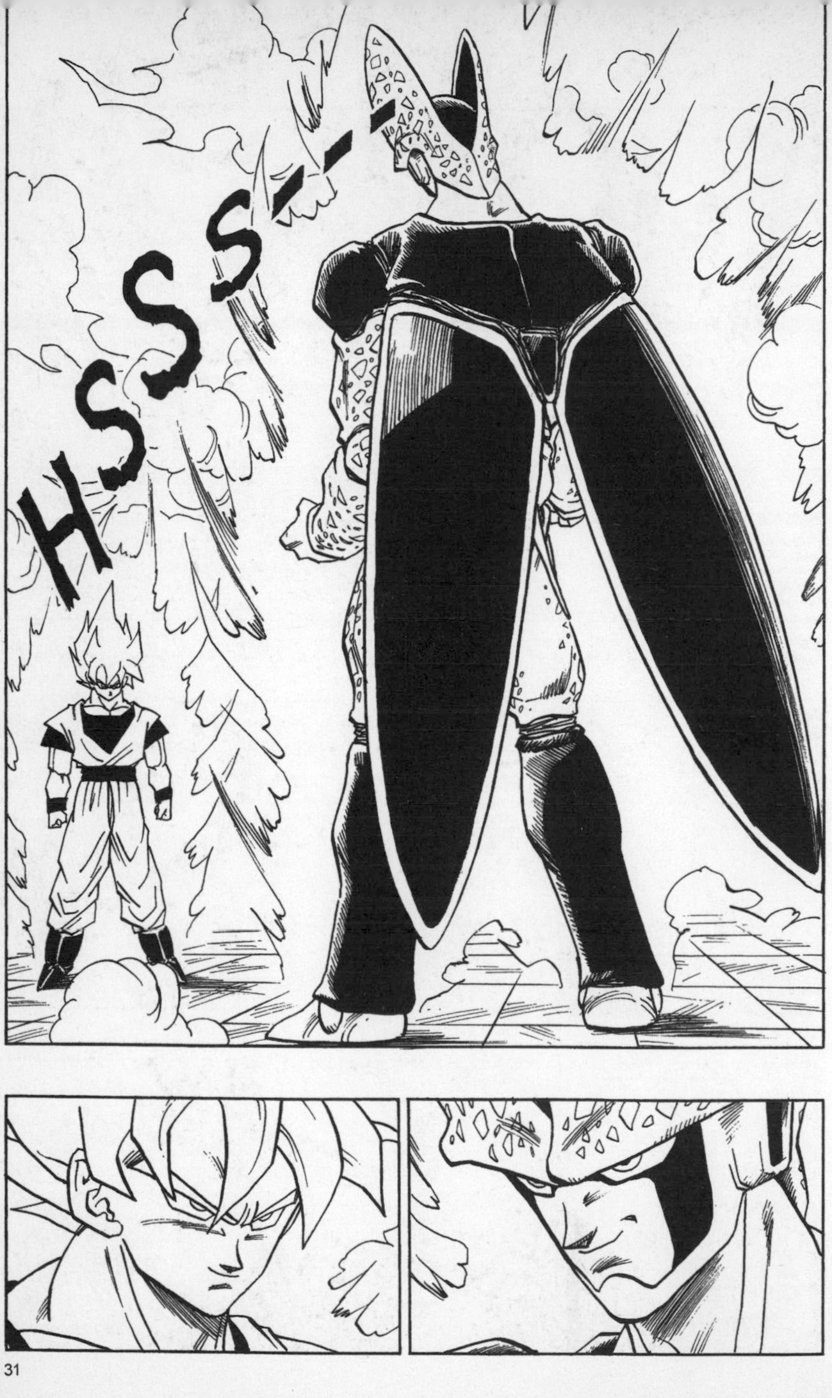

HSSS--

READ
THIS
WAY

THE SAME THING... HAPPENED TO CELL... ?!
...M-MUST BE A POPULAR TRICK...

Zp

ZK

DO IT.

OK.

ZB

KOW

THOG

READ THIS WAY

WOK

READ THIS WAY

NEXT: The Summit of Battle

DBZ:205 • The Highest Level

READ THIS WAY

SHP

KA...
ME...

GAK!

WAIT !!!
DON'T SHOOT A KAME-HAMEHA WHILE YOU'RE REVVED THAT HIGH!

HA...
ME...

BMM

H-
HE'S
GOING
TO...
!

HAAAH
!

READ
THIS
WAY

!!
ZD
CELL, OVER HERE !!!

READ THIS WAY
KYOW

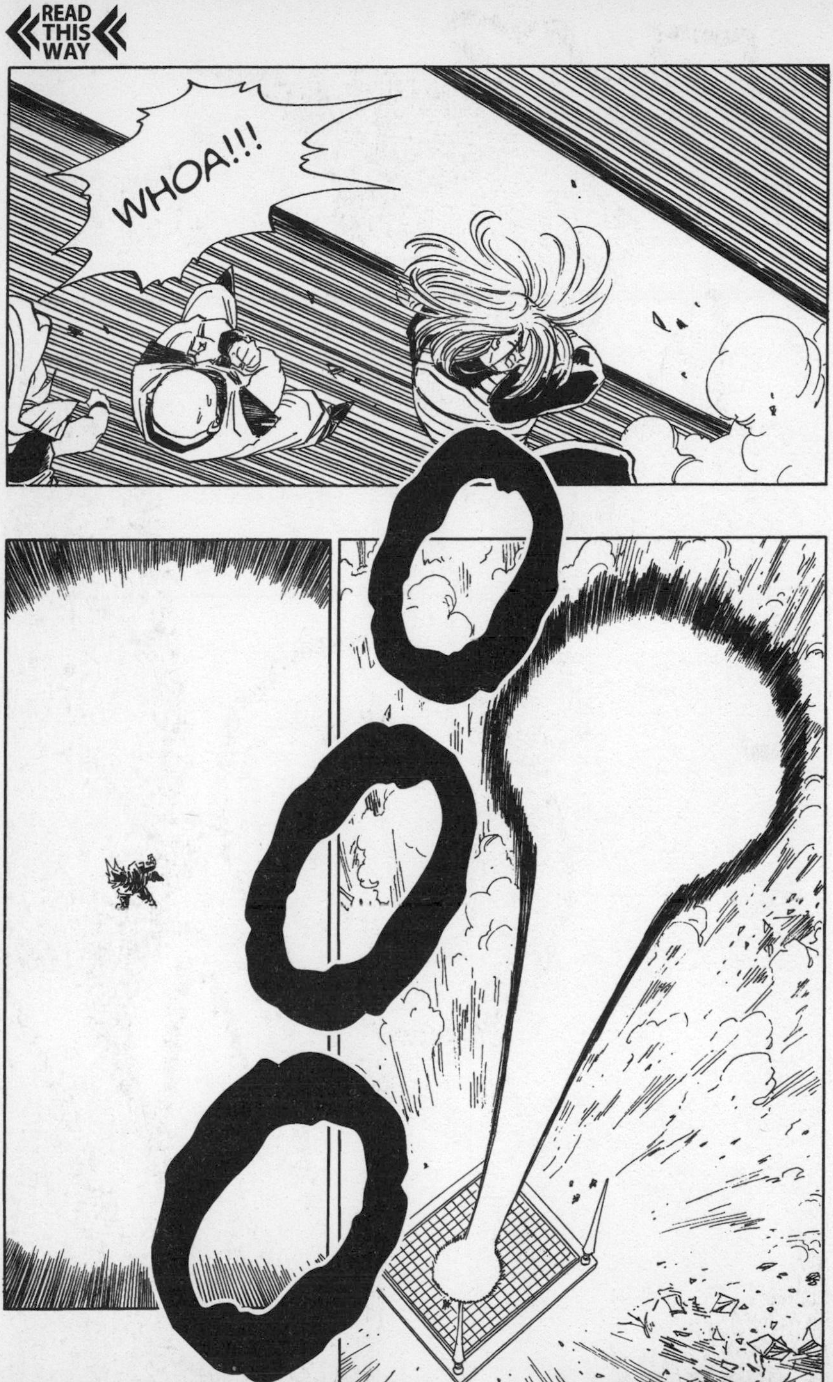

READ THIS WAY

WHOA!!!

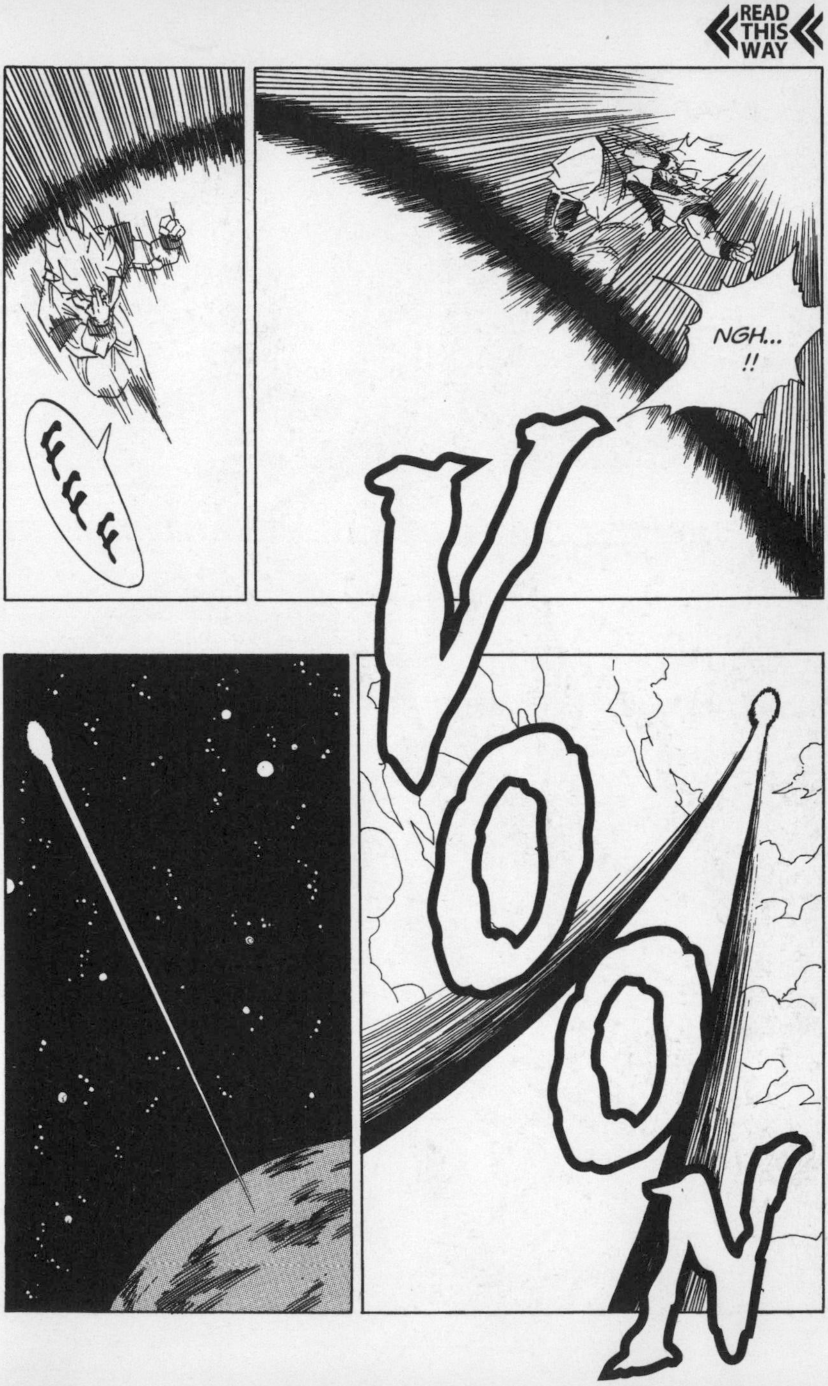

NGH... !!

VOOON

...!!

WHAT ?!

DOK

READ
THIS
WAY

DOM
TP
...

READ THIS WAY

HWOOO

PHEW...

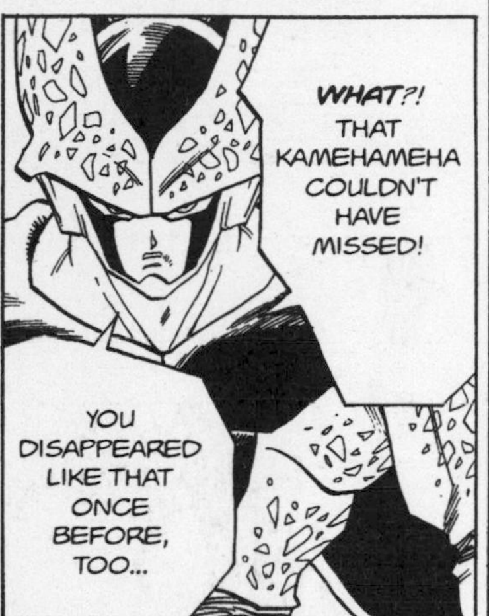
WHAT?! THAT KAMEHAMEHA COULDN'T HAVE MISSED!
YOU DISAPPEARED LIKE THAT ONCE BEFORE, TOO...

I CAN TELE- PORT.
GUESS YOU DIDN'T KNOW.

I SEE...

TELEPORT ?!
...THAT'S ANNOYING.

SO TELL ME...
WOULD YOU HAVE SHOT THAT KAMEHAMEHA AND DESTROYED THE EARTH IF I HADN'T JUMPED?

TO ANSWER YOUR QUESTION, THOUGH...

I'D DESTROY THE EARTH WITHOUT BATTING AN EYE.

IT'LL JUST COST ME A LITTLE **FUN**, THAT'S ALL.

.....

NN

!?

READ
THIS
WAY

N
VN
WOK

READ THIS WAY
VNN
UNH !!
WOK

SHP

BMM

NEXT: Defeat or Death!

D-PA-PA-PA-PA-PA..

DBZ:206 • Ring Out

READ THIS WAY

ZDD

BM

VNN

SHP

READ THIS WAY

VNN
WHOOO
!!
WHOOOSH
SHP

IT WOULD BE A SHAME TO END THIS FIGHT WITH AN OUT-OF-BOUNDS.

HUH?

EVERYBODY!

GET AWAY FROM THE RING!!!

ARRGH!!!

READ THIS WAY

ZMM

DWOOM

READ THIS WAY

RRRRMMMMM...

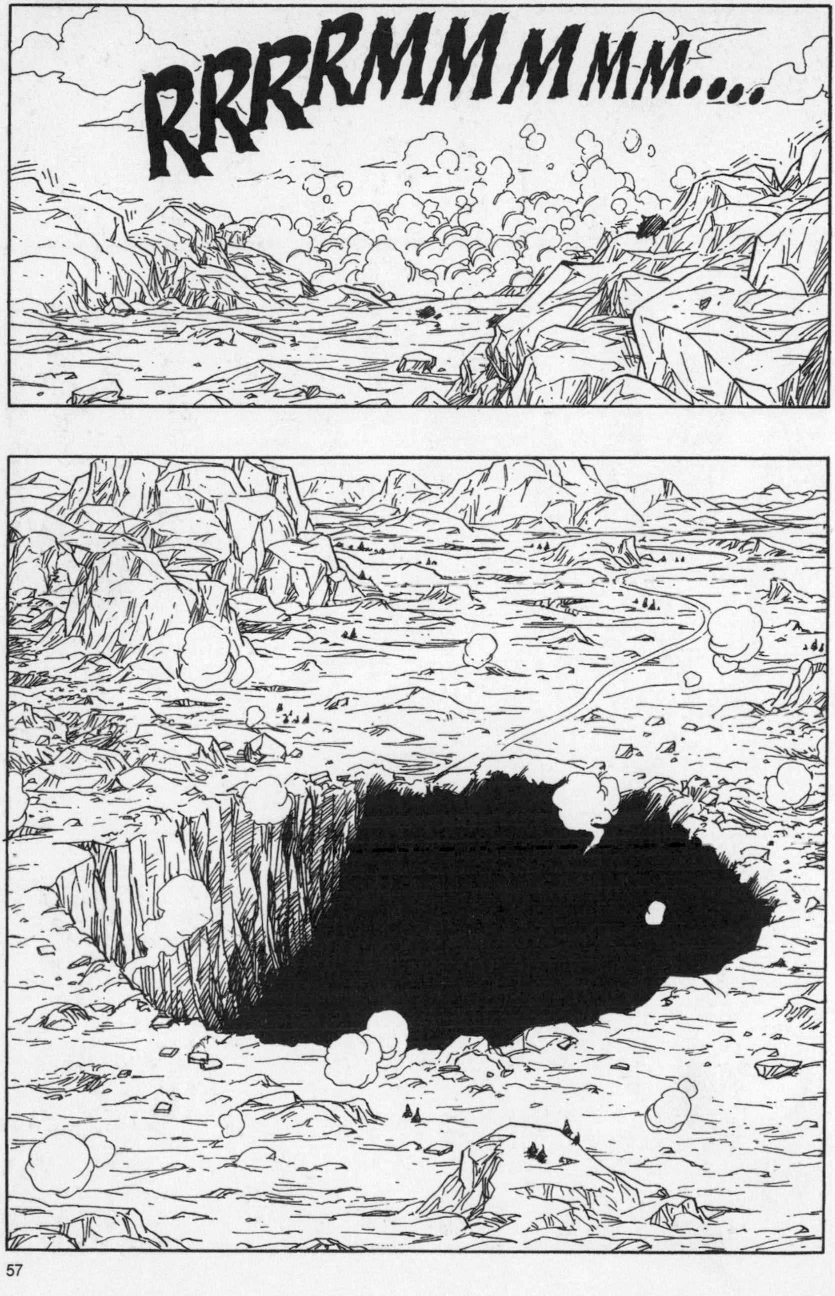

READ THIS WAY

PHEW !
THAT WAS CLOSE... !

TH-THANK YOU...

YOU SHOULD LEAVE. YOU'RE IN THE WAY.

W-WE CAN'T DO THAT! HERCULE IS UP NEXT!
...

RIGHT ?!
OF COURSE !!
BUT MAYBE WE SHOULD STEP BACK A BIT FURTHER...

NOW THE WHOLE EARTH IS THE RING.

ONE OF US WILL HAVE TO ADMIT DEFEAT... OR DIE.

RIGHT.

SO YOU WANT TO SEE THIS TO THE END.

NOW THEN...

I BETTER USE ALL THIS NEW SPACE.

HOO

D

M

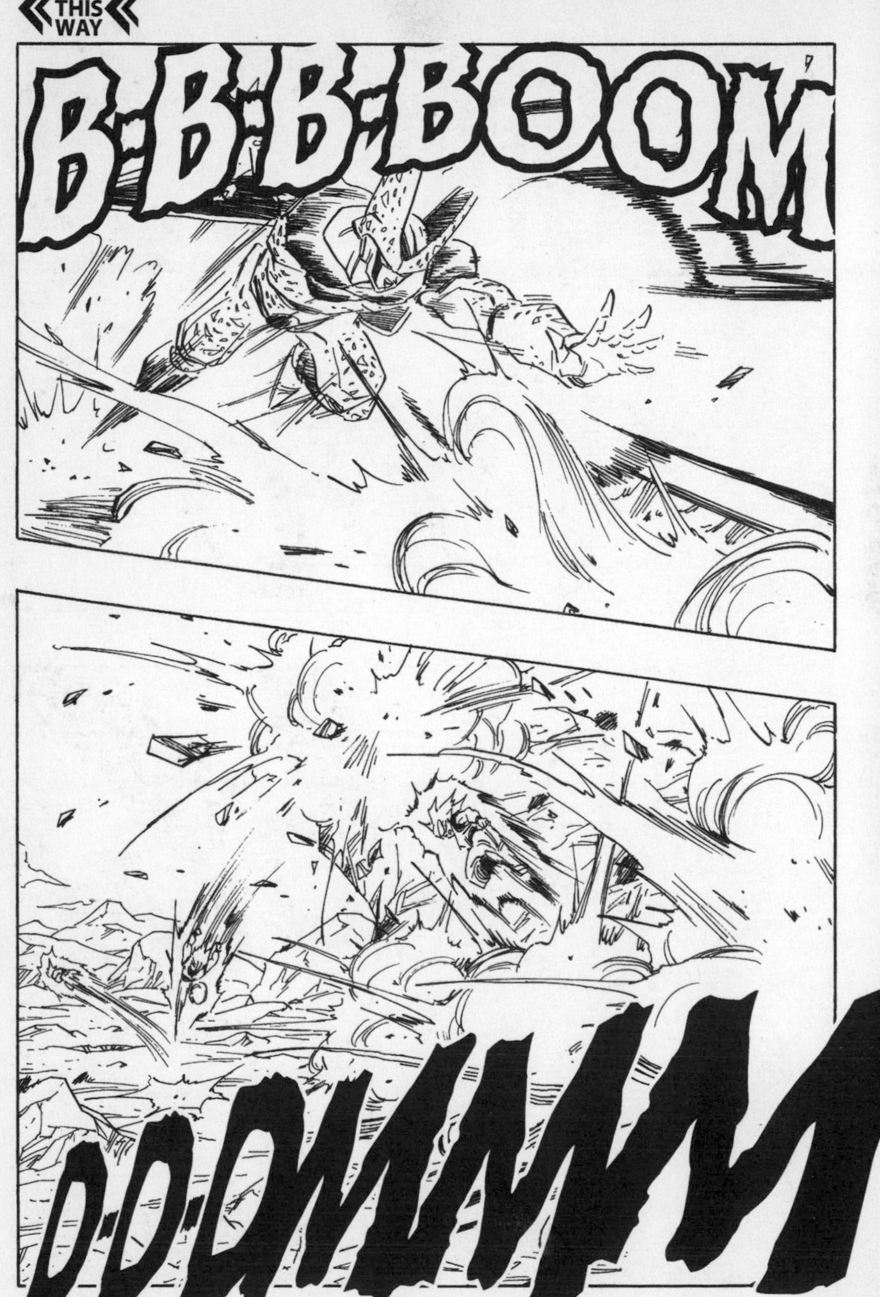
READ THIS WAY
B-B-B-BOOM

BOOM BOOM

READ THIS WAY

FWAH

KA...
ME...
HA...

HA HA HA HA!! YOU DON'T DARE UNLEASH IT FROM UP THERE!!
YOU KNOW WHAT THAT WOULD DO TO THE EARTH!!

ME...

H-HEY...!

DBZ:207
Kamehameha Full Power

READ THIS WAY

THE KAME-HAME-HA!!!
CAN GOKU TRULY BE PLANNING TO UNLEASH IT AT FULL POWER?!

READ
THIS
WAY

H-HE WON'T DO IT... !!
NOT WITH THE EARTH IN HIS LINE OF FIRE!!

...WHAT ARE YOU DOING... ?
THERE'S NO WAY YOU'D EVER...

...!
OR IS THERE ?!

HE'S DOING IT...!!!

!!

FFT

OH...

READ
THIS
WAY

HAH
!!!!!
ZMM

READ
THIS
WAY

GLARH
!!!!!!
WOOM

READ
THIS
WAY

Z-Z-Z-ZMM

HUF!
HUF!
HUF!

READ
THIS
WAY

Y-
YES!!!
HE
DID
IT
!!!
OF
COURSE!!
HE
TELE-
PORTED
!!

WE WON!!
HA HA
HAH!!

WHAT'S
WRONG...
?
WHY
AREN'T
YOU
HAPPY
?

......

W-WELL,
HERCULE! IT
APPEARS
THAT HE'S
BEATEN
CELL!!
......

READ
THIS
WAY

UH... NOT BAD !
OF COURSE, I'M SORRY I DIDN'T GET TO FINISH IT MYSELF!

...WHAT'S GOING ON... ?
EVEN AFTER THAT... THERE'S STILL SO MUCH CHI LEFT...
HUF
HUF

WATCH OUT, GOKU !!
CELL'S GONNA COME BACK !!

WHAT ?!

VNN

FBB

!!

GGGGG...

GGGG...

GLOOB

READ THIS WAY

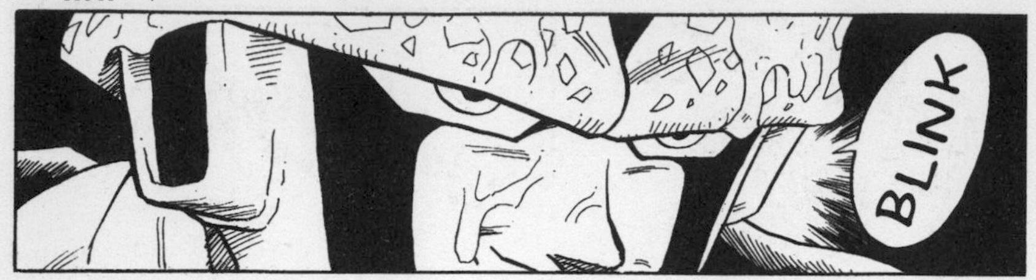
BLINK

GNG GNG

I-IT CAME BACK TO LIFE...!!
EEE-EEK!

OH, RIGHT. YOU CAN REGEN-ERATE.
OF COURSE... JUST LIKE PICCOLO!

I KNOW THAT!!

BM

YOU DO?!

BM

NEXT: Why, Goku, Why?

DBZ:208 • Last Resort

HYAH-
HYAH-
HYAH
!!!!

D-D-D-DM

READ
THIS
WAY

DOOM
UNH
!!!!

D.D.D.DM
DYAH-
DYAH-
DYAH
!!!!

DAH-
DAH-
DAH
!!!!

READ THIS WAY

D-D-D-DM
YEEK !!!
RR... RRG... !!!
KRAK
BAH !!!!!

VNNN

READ THIS WAY

HUF!
HUF!

HUF
HUF
VNNN
HUF

SHOOT...

WELL. YOU MADE ME RESORT TO A FORCE FIELD. I'M IMPRESSED.
I DIDN'T THINK YOU COULD BE SO DESTRUC-TIVE.

OH...
MAN...

TH-THIS ISN'T A MOVIE...?
GULP

READ THIS WAY

AIN'T THAT CHI-CHI'S HUSBAND?! AH TOLD YEW HE BLEACHED HIS HAIR!
SURELY DOES LOOK LIKE 'IM...
HE ALWAYS DID DRESS KINDA PECULIAR...

BLAST IT!!
HE WAS SO CLOSE !!
...NO HE WASN'T...
IT LOOKS LIKE HE'S PUTTING UP A GOOD FIGHT.
BUT HE'S DESPERATE... AND CELL ISN'T.
WHAT ?!
Y-YOU MEAN... ?

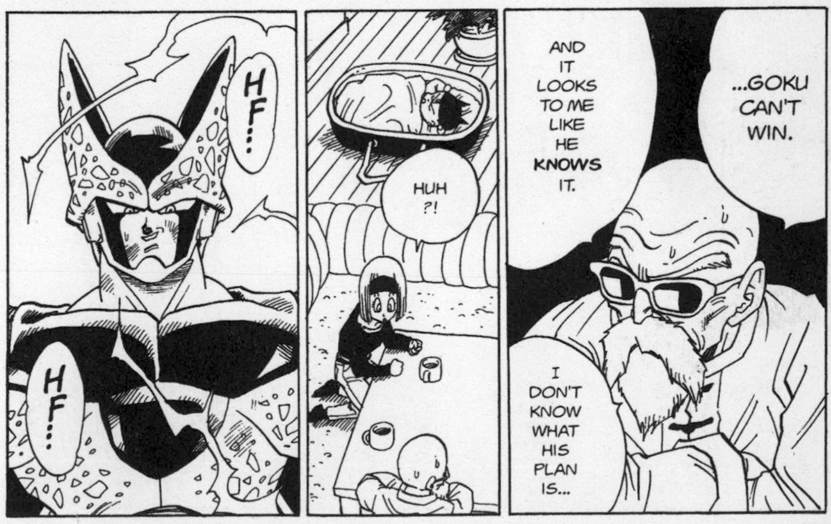
...GOKU CAN'T WIN.
AND IT LOOKS TO ME LIKE HE KNOWS IT.
I DON'T KNOW WHAT HIS PLAN IS...
HUH ?!
HF...
HF...

READ THIS WAY

FT

HUF!
HUF!
HUF!

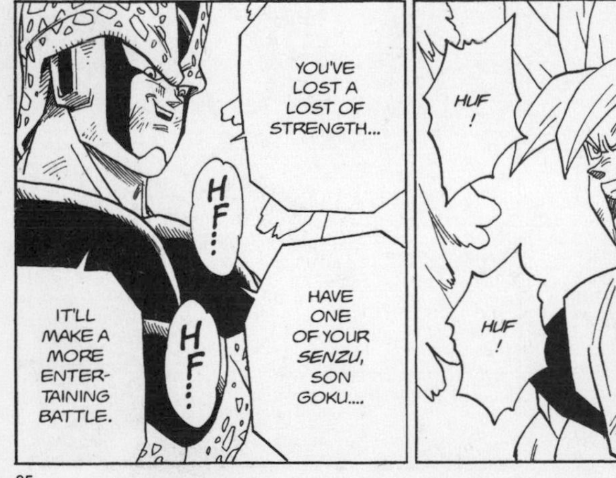
YOU'VE LOST A LOST OF STRENGTH...
HF...
HAVE ONE OF YOUR SENZU, SON GOKU....
HF...
IT'LL MAKE A MORE ENTER-TAINING BATTLE.

READ THIS WAY

......
HFF
HFF

IT'S RIGHT !!
WE SHOULD GIVE GOKU A *SENZU*, AND ALL TURN ON CELL—IT'S WEAKENED ENOUGH BY NOW!!

...
KURIRIN! HURRY, GET HIM THE *SENZU*...!!

SHUT UP, TRUNKS !!
!!

I GUESS YOU DON'T HAVE A SAIYAN'S PRIDE.
I'M SURE HE'D RATHER CHOOSE DEATH THAN WIN THAT WAY.
HE'S NO LONGER FIGHTING JUST TO SAVE THE EARTH. REMEMBER THAT.

...
BUT... AT THIS RATE...

YES. HE'LL DEFINITELY LOSE.

READ
THIS
WAY

I HATE THE THOUGHT, BUT I'LL ADMIT IT. I'VE TRAINED HARD, BUT I COULD NEVER BEAT KAKARROT. HE'S BRILLIANT.
UNFORTUNATELY, CELL WASN'T JUST ONE, BUT **TWO** STEPS AHEAD OF HIM.

B-BUT WHAT CAN WE DO...?!
JUST STAND BY AND **WATCH**?!

YOU SAID YOURSELF THAT HE MUST HAVE A PLAN.
PIN YOUR HOPES ON THAT...

...

HEH HEH... WHAT'S WRONG? DOES YOUR PRIDE PREVENT YOU FROM TAKING THE *SENZU?*
I'VE SPENT SO MUCH OF MY ENERGY. IF YOU COME BACK UP TO FULL POWER YOUR CHANCES WILL INCREASE... **SLIGHTLY**.
COME ON. I WANT TO HAVE MORE FUN!

READ
THIS
WAY

HUF!
HUF!

HEH!!

FFT

HEY...

I
LOSE.

!!

WH-

WHAT?!

HE'S GIVING UP...?!

N—

NO—!!

WHAT...

....IS HE *THINKING* ?!

READ THIS WAY

WHAT? WH-WHAT DID HE JUST SAY?!
IT SOUNDED LIKE HE SAID... HE'S GIVING UP!

...SON GOKU...
DO YOU REALIZE WHAT THOSE WORDS MEAN...?

ONCE NO ONE IS LEFT TO FIGHT IN THE CELL GAME...
...EVERY LAST PERSON ON EARTH WILL DIE.

DON'T GET THE WRONG IDEA.
WE HAVEN'T RUN OUT OF FIGHTERS YET.

IT'S THE SAME THING.
VEGETA AND TRUNKS MAY HAVE IMPROVED, BUT THEY'RE NOTHING LIKE YOU.

NEXT: The One Who Surpasses Goku

DBZ:209 • The Successor

THE CELL GAME WILL END IN THIS NEXT MATCH.
BECAUSE IF *HE* LOSES, THERE'LL BE NOBODY ELSE WHO CAN BEAT YOU.
WH-WHO *IS* IT? I CAN'T STAND THE SUSPENSE!!

READ THIS WAY

DO YOU MEAN TO TELL ME THERE'S SOMEONE STRONGER THAN YOU... **AND** ME?!
YUP.

HEH HEH HEH.
LET ME HEAR THE NAME OF THIS FANTASY WARRIOR, HM?

READ THIS WAY

H-HE'S GOING TO SAY "HERCULE"... !
T-TELL HIM I HAVE A STOMACHACHE AND I CAN'T FIGHT!!
HE'S ABOUT TO SAY IT...!

UP

READ THIS WAY

YOU'RE UP...
GOHAN!!

!!

WHAT?!

HUH?!

READ THIS WAY

WHAT...
DID HE SAY... ?!

!!

HAS HE LOST HIS MIND AT LAST?!
IS HE GOING TO SEND HIS OWN SON TO HIS DEATH ?!

"GOHAN"... THAT MEANS RICE!
WHAT ?!

ASTOUNDING... THEY'RE TAKING A LUNCH BREAK!
HOW CAN THEY BE SO CASUAL ?!

READ THIS WAY

VMM

TM

GIVE ME A BREAK...
LITTLE **SON GOHAN**... ?!

YOU CAN DO IT.
RIGHT, GOHAN ?
ME... FIGHT **CELL**... ?

COME TO YOUR SENSES, GOKU! HOW CAN HE DO THIS?!
HE'S GROWN REMARKABLY, BUT THIS IS CELL— AGAINST WHOM NOT EVEN YOU STOOD A CHANCE !!

READ THIS WAY

PICCOLO. GOHAN HAS MORE POWER THAN I CAN BELIEVE.
THINK ABOUT IT. HE'S BEEN FIGHTING WITH US EVER SINCE HE WAS LITTLE. I WAS NOTHING LIKE THIS WHEN I WAS HIS AGE!

B-BUT EVEN IF HE'S SUPER SAIYAN NOW...
...TO FIGHT CELL... !

THE POWER SLEEPING DEEP WITHIN HIM BEGAN TO AWAKEN IN THE ROOM OF SPIRIT AND TIME.
SHALL I ASK HIM HOW HE FEELS ?

WHAT DO YOU SAY, GOHAN? WAS OUR BATTLE TOO TOUGH FOR YOU?
...

WELL... NO...
...B-BUT NEITHER OF YOU WAS FIGHTING FOR REAL YET, RIGHT?!

I DON'T KNOW ABOUT CELL, BUT I WAS DOING MY BEST.
SO TO YOU IT LOOKED LIKE I WASN'T REALLY TRYING, HUH?
...

READ
THIS
WAY

IS...
IS THAT TRUE, GOHAN... ?!

NOD
Y-YEAH...

!!

I-IMPOSSIBLE... !
THE BRAT'S LYING !

HMPH !

PAT

DO IT, GOHAN !
BRING PEACE BACK TO THE WORLD.
YOU WANT TO GROW UP AND BE A SCIENTIST, DON'T YOU?

ALL... ALL RIGHT...

I'LL GIVE IT A TRY...

TUG

DMM

VAH

TUP

READ THIS WAY

KURIRIN, YOU HAVE SOME SENZU, RIGHT?
COULD I HAVE ONE?
HUH? OH, SURE...

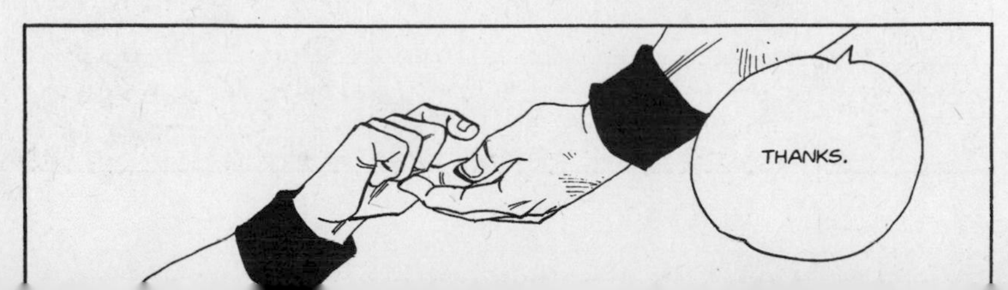
THANKS.

HF
HF

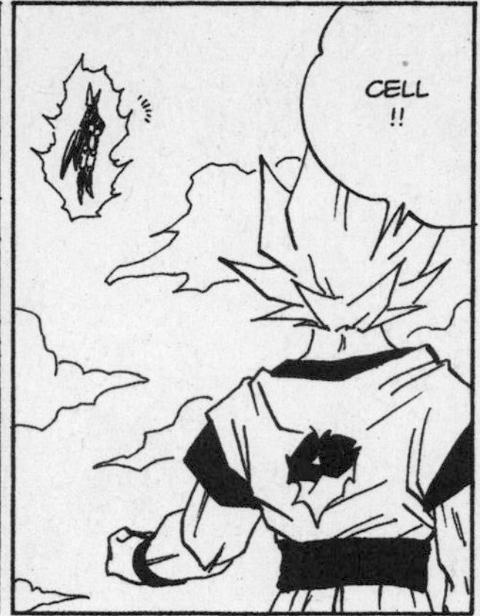
CELL !!

VIP
HEY !

SNAP

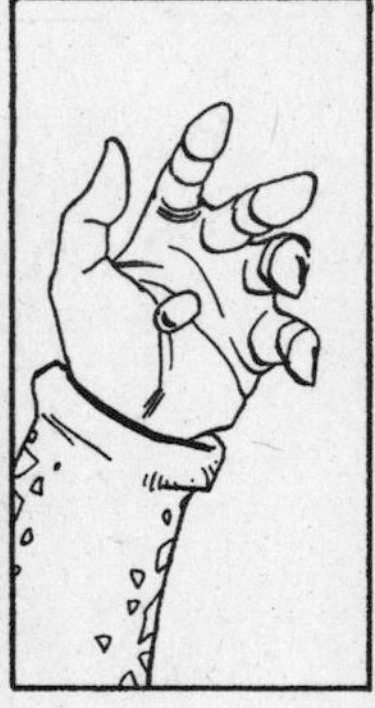

THAT'S A SENZU. EAT IT!
WH-WHAT THE... ?!

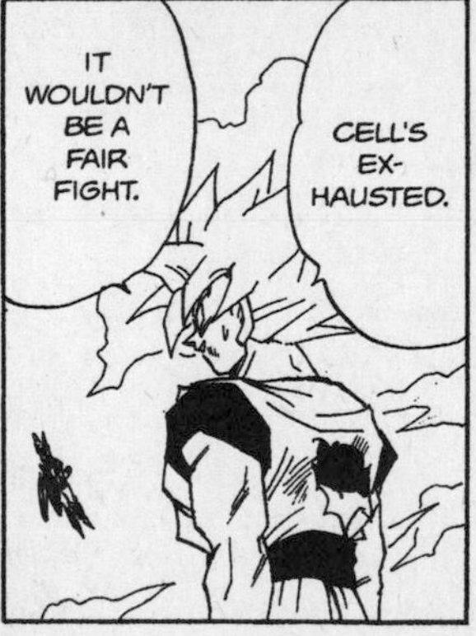
CELL'S EX-HAUSTED.
IT WOULDN'T BE A FAIR FIGHT.

WHO CARES ABOUT *FAIR* ?!

YOU FOOL. ALWAYS THE HERO.
YOU DON'T GET THAT THIS WILL BE YOUR DOOM, DO YOU?

READ THIS WAY

I WON'T DECLINE, OF COURSE. AND YOU'LL SOON REGRET IT.

MUNCH

GLP

I SEE...
!

THESE *ARE* GOOD
!

DMM

READ THIS WAY

!!

!!

DBZ: 210 • Let's Go, Gohan!

READ THIS WAY

READ
THIS
WAY

TH-
THAT'S
GOHAN...
?!
...MILD-
MANNERED
GOHAN...
?!

H-HOW DID
THAT BRAT
GET SO
POWERFUL?!
I DON'T
BELIEVE
MY EYES!!

PERHAPS
WHAT
SON
GOKU
SAID...
...WASN'T
JUST
A
BLUFF
AFTER
ALL
!
BUT STILL...
IT'S A JOKE
TO SAY THAT
HE CAN
DEFEAT ME!

I'LL KILL
HIM
BEFORE
HE CAN
LAND A
BLOW!!
WEEP, SON GOKU!!
WEEP WHEN YOUR
SON DIES BECAUSE
OF YOUR
ARROGANCE!!

READ
THIS
WAY

SSs---

TP

SHP

CON-
CEITED
WHELP...
YOU
THINK
YOU CAN
DO
THIS...
?

YOU MIGHT
BE LUCKY. YOU'LL
DIE BEFORE
YOU HAVE A
CHANCE TO
DISCOVER
TRUE
TERROR!

READ THIS WAY

VIP

WSH

HNRR
!!

KYUU

!

VIP

TAH
!

READ THIS WAY

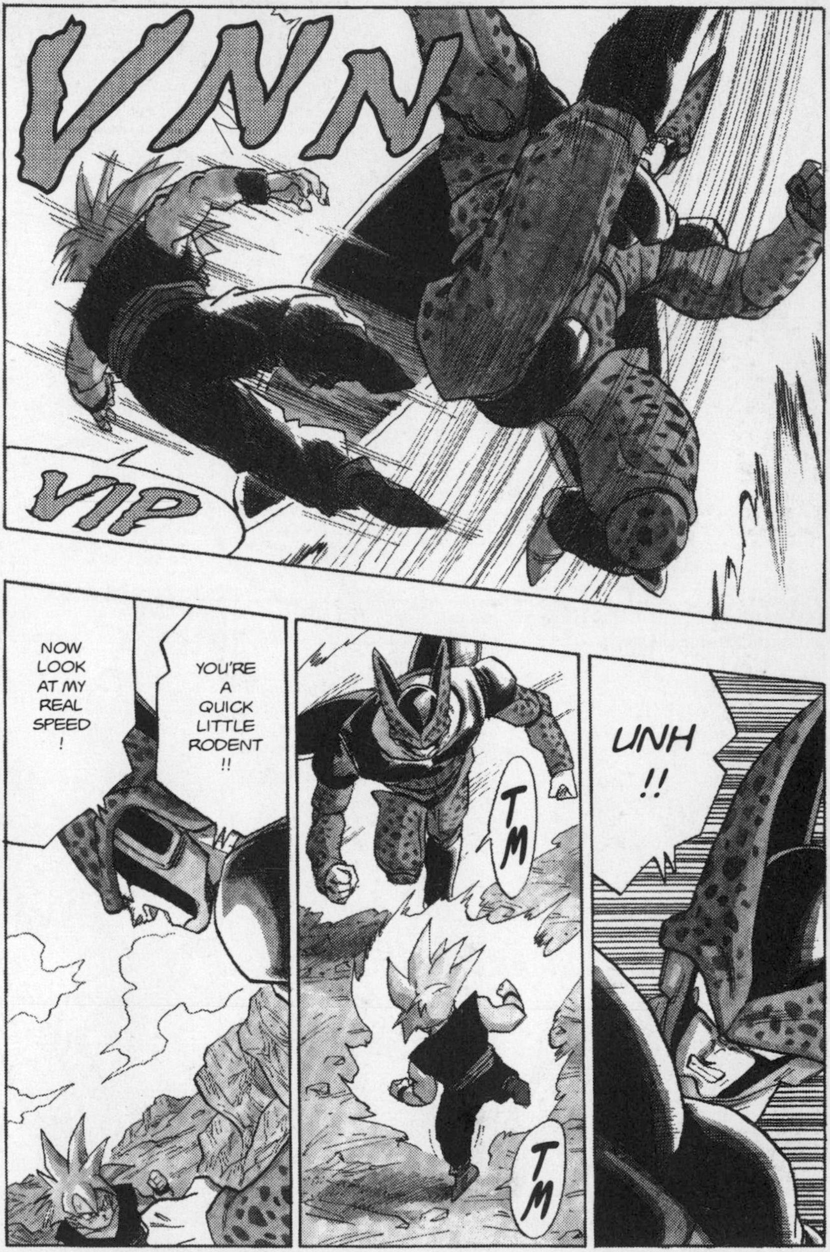

VNN

VIP

UNH !!

TM
TM

YOU'RE A QUICK LITTLE RODENT !!
NOW LOOK AT MY REAL SPEED !

READ
THIS
WAY

BMM
SNAG
KSSH
WOK

BM

BOKKA BOKKA
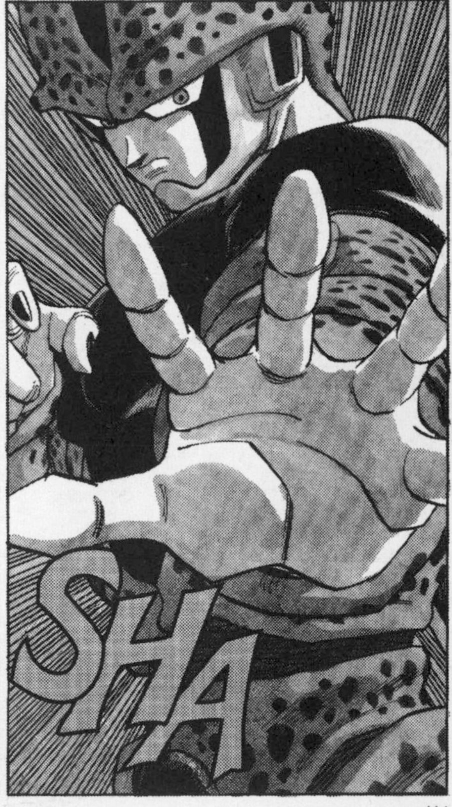
SHA

HYA
AAH
!!!!!

DOOOM

READ THIS WAY

KROKKK
WOK

READ THIS WAY

KARA KARA TMMM

IT'S HORRIBLE—!!
G-GOHAN—!!

I GUESS I OVERDID IT...
HEH HEH. HOW IMMATURE OF ME.

TMM
CHI-CHI !!
BE STRONG !!

READ THIS WAY

...

THIS IS A TRAGEDY...! JUST WHEN THEY WERE ABOUT TO BREAK FOR LUNCH, A BOY RECKLESSLY CHALLENGED CELL...
...AND LOST HIS YOUNG LIFE...

...GOKU... THIS IS YOUR FAULT...
YOUR JUDGMENT WAS WRONG...
EVERY-ONE WARNED YOU...

YOU KILLED GOHAN !!!

DON'T JUMP TO CON-CLUSIONS, PICCOLO.
CAN'T YOU STILL FEEL GOHAN'S CHI?

WHOA...
H-HE'S RIGHT... !!

READ THIS WAY

SON GOKU!! ENOUGH OF THESE GAMES!
EAT YOUR SENZU AND FIGHT ME ONCE MORE!!

IDIOT!
LOOK BEHIND YOU!

WHAT?

READ THIS WAY

!!

...WHAT A SURPRISE...
YOU'RE TOUGHER THAN I THOUGHT.

L-LET'S NOT DO THIS...
...THIS BATTLE IS POINTLESS...

HUH ?!

HA HA! OF ALL THE THINGS TO SAY!
THE CELL GAME HAS NO POINT?

SURE IT DOES! I'M HAVING FUN, AND YOU'RE TRYING TO SAVE ALL HUMANITY!

READ THIS WAY

BUT I DON'T LIKE TO FIGHT... LIKE DAD DOES.
I DON'T WANT TO KILL ANY-BODY...

...NOT EVEN SOMEBODY AS AWFUL AS YOU.

WHAT'S GOHAN SAYING...? I CAN'T MAKE IT OUT...

...OK, SO YOU DON'T LIKE TO FIGHT.
BUT WHAT'S THIS NONSENSE ABOUT NOT WANTING TO KILL *ME?*

READ THIS WAY

YOU COULDN'T KILL ME IN A HUNDRED YEARS! AM I WRONG?

I'M... BEGINNING TO UNDER-STAND...
...WHY DAD SAID ONLY I CAN DEFEAT YOU.

EVER SINCE I WAS LITTLE... WHEN I GET MAD, I LOSE CONTROL AND GO BERSERK.
...I THINK... THAT'S WHAT DAD'S COUNTING ON...

...
OH *REALLY*... ?

WELL, YOUR PLAN FAILED.

WHAT ?!

READ THIS WAY

DID YOU THINK I WOULD GET COLD FEET IF YOU TOLD ME THAT?! YOU STILL THINK LIKE A KID!
NOW I REALLY WANT TO SEE YOU MAD!!
!!
WAK

DBZ: 211 • The Rage of Son Gohan?

READ THIS WAY

THOG
GAH... !!!
VOK!

READ THIS WAY

COME ON!! GET MAD!!!
SHOW ME YOUR TRUE POWERS!!!

TM

READ
THIS
WAY

WOK
CELL FELL ON ITS BUTT...!!!
ZMM

READ
THIS
WAY

PLIP

...

WSH

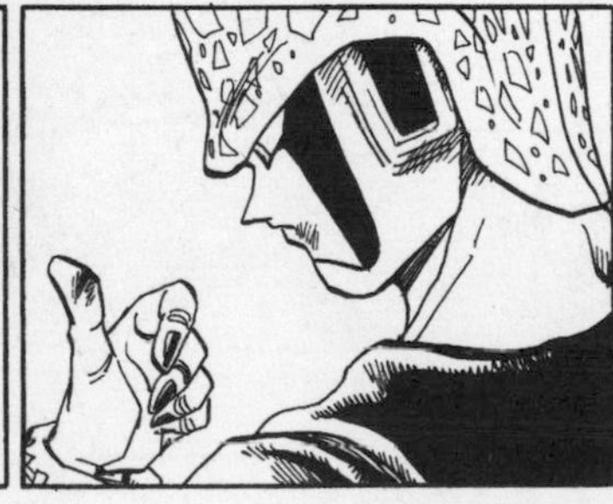

RUB RUB

HEH
ONE WAY OR ANOTHER... I'LL FIND YOUR RAGE !

READ
THIS
WAY

THAT'S IT, CELL! MAKE GOHAN MAD!!
THEN YOU'LL KNOW FEAR FOR THE FIRST TIME IN YOUR LIFE!

SHHH

READ THIS WAY

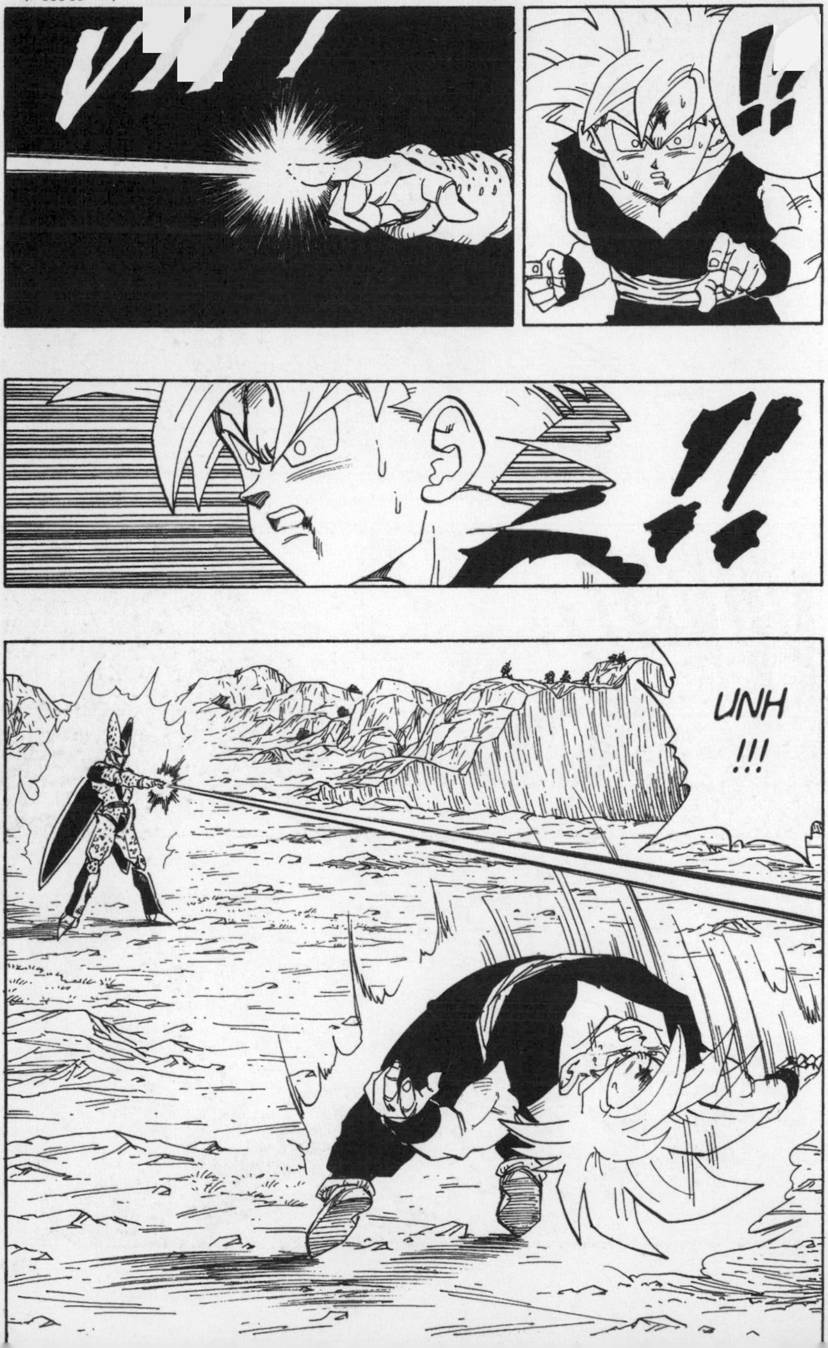

UNH
!!!

READ THIS WAY

VIII

BZZ

TH-THAT'S...
...THE MOVE FREEZA USED !!

VVVIIIII

BZZT
BZZT
BZZ

READ THIS WAY

BZZT

GOMP

!!

READ THIS WAY

NNNGG

MMRII

MMG

GGG

AGH...!!! GAAH... !!!!

READ THIS WAY

I CAN'T STOMACH ANY MORE OF THIS !!
I DON'T CARE WHAT YOU SAY!! I'M GOING TO HELP GOHAN !!!

PICCOLO, WAIT!! YOU DON'T STAND A CHANCE!!
WAIT JUST A LITTLE LONGER!!

YOU WANT ME TO WAIT?! FOR WHAT ?!
WAIT FOR GOHAN TO BE KILLED ?!

NO. WAIT FOR HIM TO GET MAD.
RAGE WILL UNLEASH HIS TRUE POWER. THEN WE'LL REALLY SEE SOMETHING.

WHAT ?!

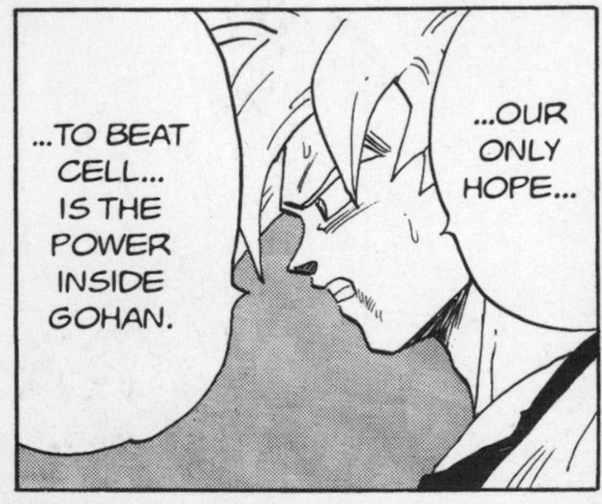
...OUR ONLY HOPE...
...TO BEAT CELL... IS THE POWER INSIDE GOHAN.

READ THIS WAY

...

WH- WHAT...?! THAT BRAT HAS THAT MUCH POWER...?

NNG... GAH...
MEK MEK
AREN'T YOU ANGRY YET?!
I KNOW THIS HURTS!! YOUR ANGER IS BUBBLING UP!!

GOKU, YOU'RE MISTAKEN. YOUR SON DOES NOT HAVE YOUR WARRIOR'S STOMACH!!
DOES HE EVEN KNOW ABOUT THIS PLAN? DID YOU DISCUSS IT WITH HIM FIRST?!

...

DO YOU KNOW WHAT'S IN GOHAN'S MIND RIGHT NOW?! WELL, IT'S NOT RAGE!!
HE'S THINKING, "WHY WON'T DAD HELP ME WHEN I'M IN SO MUCH PAIN?!"

READ
THIS
WAY

"DOES HE CARE MORE ABOUT THE RULES OF THIS FIGHT THAN MY *LIFE?!*"
HOWEVER STRONG HE MAY BE, HE'S STILL A CHILD !!
I DON'T CARE IF I DIE!! I'M GOING !!

KURIRIN, GIVE ME A SENZU !!
Y-YOU GOT IT!!

THDD

READ
THIS
WAY

!?

HFF*
HFF*
HFF*
HFF*

...?!

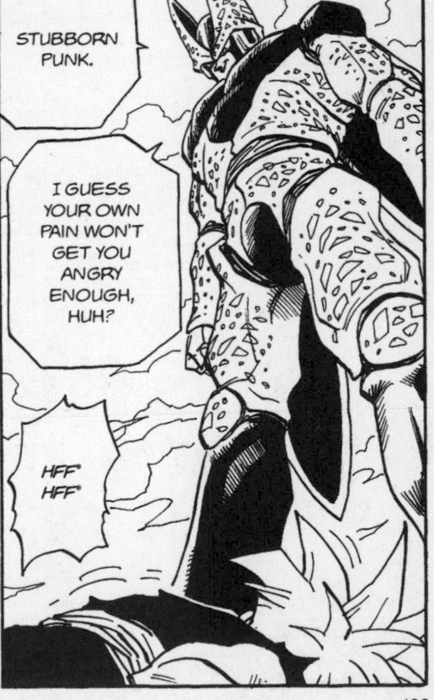
STUBBORN PUNK.
I GUESS YOUR OWN PAIN WON'T GET YOU ANGRY ENOUGH, HUH?
HFF*
HFF*

...IN THAT CASE, I'LL ASK YOUR FRIENDS FOR SOME ASSIST-ANCE.

!!

NEXT: Revenge of the Android!

DBZ:212 • #16's Secret Weapon

READ THIS WAY

THIS BAG CONTAINS THE SENZU, DOESN'T IT?
THEY'RE ANNOYING. I'LL TAKE IT.

VMM
HEY !!

OH-
NO... !!

SHMP

I DON'T NEED TO DIRTY MY OWN HANDS WITH THE LIKES OF THEM.
HEH HEH HEH.

READ THIS WAY

WHAT ?!
WHAT ARE YOU DOING ?!

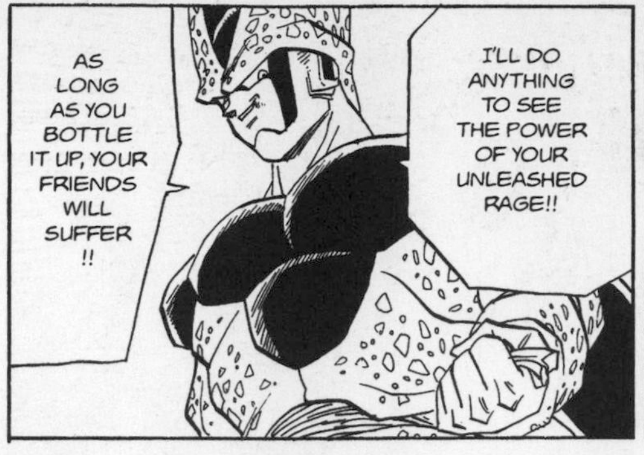
I'LL DO ANYTHING TO SEE THE POWER OF YOUR UNLEASHED RAGE!!
AS LONG AS YOU BOTTLE IT UP, YOUR FRIENDS WILL SUFFER !!

PLEASE... DON'T !!
I... I DON'T KNOW HOW TO CONTROL IT MYSELF !!
THAT'S WHY I CAN'T DO IT!!

...AND THAT'S WHY I'M GOING TO MAKE YOUR FRIENDS SUFFER.

HSS

WATCH OUT!!! IT'S UP TO SOME-THING!!
SHOOT!! I SHOULD'VE TAKEN THE SENZU WHILE I COULD !!

AAUGH... !!!

READ THIS WAY

WOK

READ
THIS
WAY

!!
WOK

READ THIS WAY

GRAB
#16 !!!

!!

WHEN DID HE GET THERE ?!
HE'S A MACHINE!! HIS ENERGY CAN GO UNDE-TECTED !

#16 IS GOING TO FIGHT CELL !!!
HE DOESN'T HAVE A CHANCE !!!

FORGIVE ME FOR SACRIFICING ALL OF YOU!
I'LL HAVE TO BLOW MYSELF UP ALONG WITH CELL !!
!!

READ THIS WAY

WH—
WHAT ?!
OH... !!

THIS IS THE FINAL POWER I WAS NEVER TO USE!!
NONE OF YOU CAN SURVIVE A BLAST AT SUCH CLOSE RANGE!!

UNH !!!
HY AAH !!!!

READ THIS WAY

OHH
!!!

SSHHH

!?

WH-
WHY...
...DIDN'T
IT
WORK...
?

16... YOU
CAN'T
BLOW
YOURSELF
UP!! WHEN
THEY FIXED
YOU AT
CAPSULE
CORP....
DR.
BRIEFS
FOUND
THIS
BOMB
HIDDEN
INSIDE
YOUR
BODY
!

HE
TOOK
IT OUT
BECAUSE
IT WAS
TOO
DANGER-
OUS!!

READ THIS WAY

...

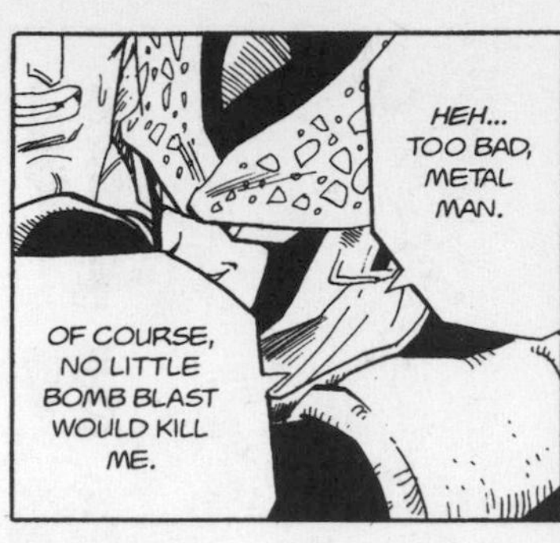
HEH... TOO BAD, METAL MAN.
OF COURSE, NO LITTLE BOMB BLAST WOULD KILL ME.

DOOM!

READ THIS WAY

URK !!!

TUMP

HA HA. I GUESS YOU WERE ONE OF DR. GERO'S FAILURES.

!!
BWOK

READ
THIS
WAY

KONG

YEEK
!!!
ROLL

NOW
IT'S
YOUR
TURN.
1... 2...
3... 4...
7 IN
ALL...
ALL
RIGHT...

READ
THIS
WAY

GG

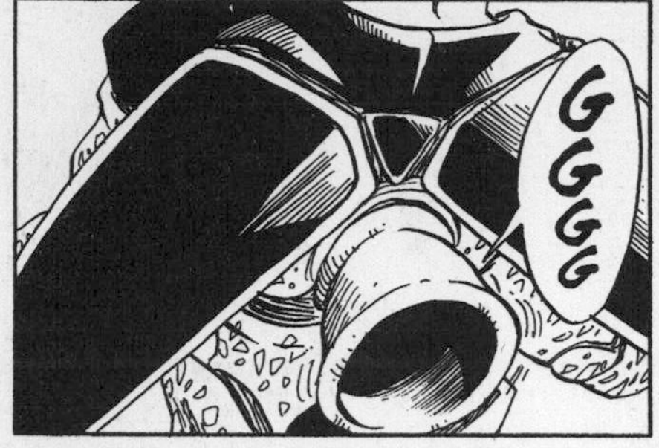
GGGG

NOW WHAT'S HE DOING... ?!

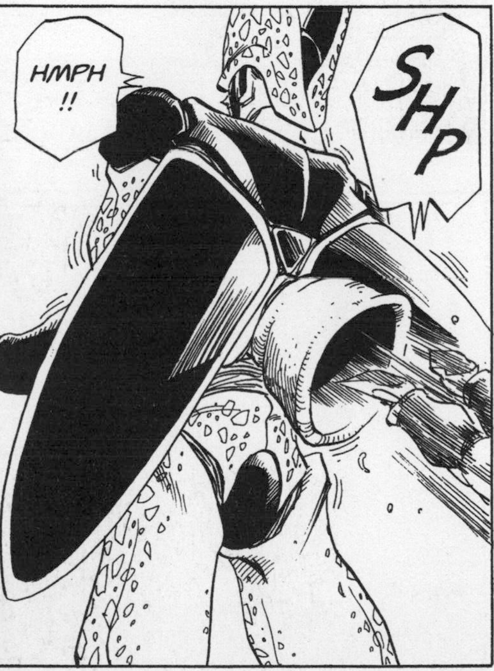
SHP
HMPH !!

SHP-SHP-SHP

!!

SQUIRM SQUIRM

KEE... KEE...

!!

KREEE!

NEXT: The Children from Hell

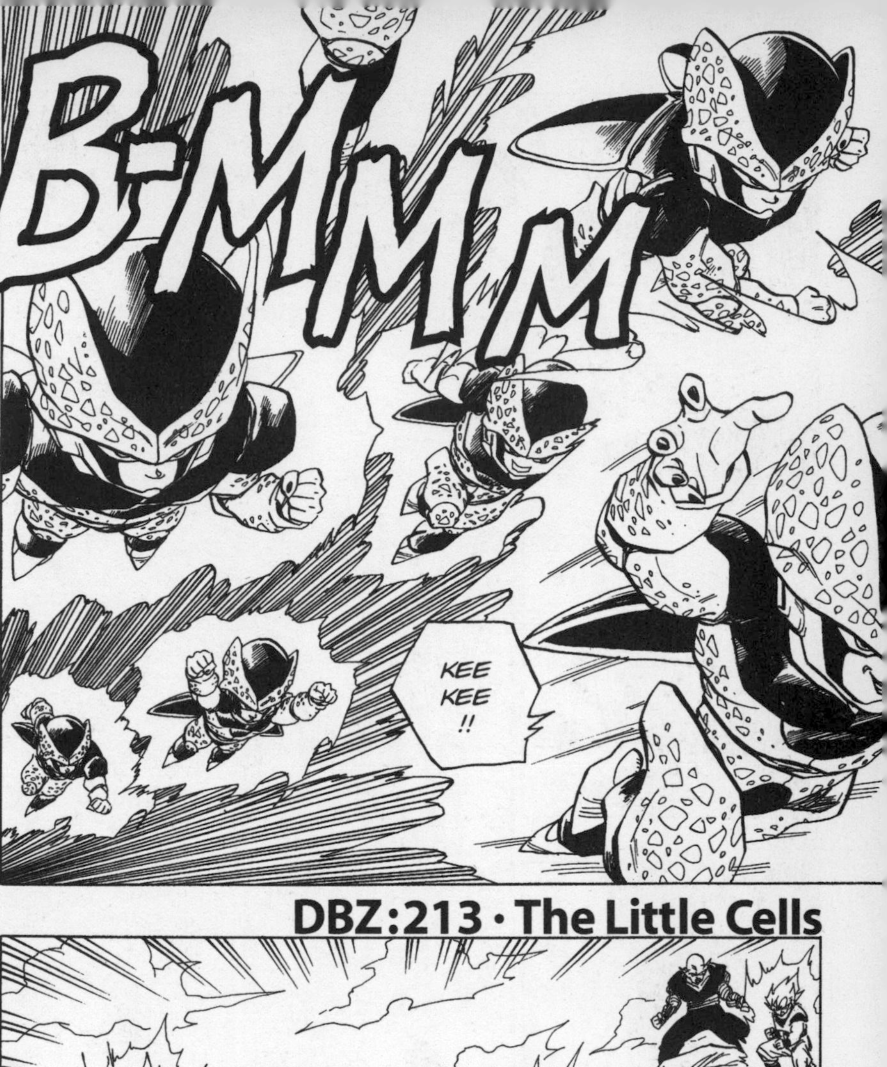

B-MMM

KEE KEE !!

DBZ:213 • The Little Cells

READ
THIS
WAY

NO, NOT THAT!

KILL THEM!!!!

D-DMM
!!

WH-
WHAT NOW?!!

HOO!
VNN

READ THIS WAY

READ THIS WAY

S-
STOP
IT...
EVERYONE BUT TRUNKS HAS DIED BEFORE... THE DRAGON BALLS CAN'T BRING THEM BACK TO LIFE ANYMORE...

TOK
TOK

HEE! HEE!
VWOK

YEE!
ZOG

BRRR

READ THIS WAY

HO!

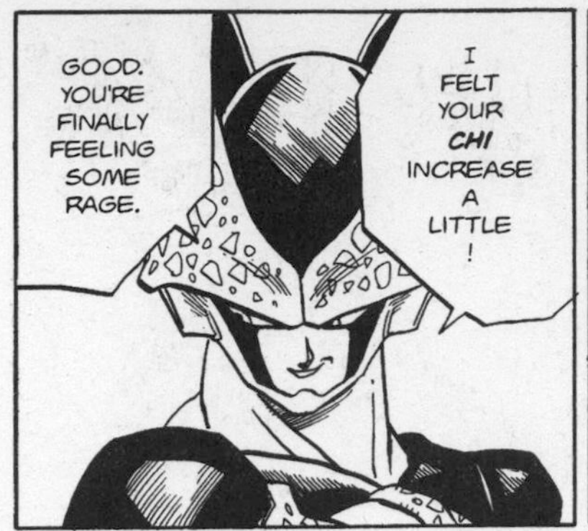
I FELT YOUR CHI INCREASE A LITTLE!
GOOD. YOU'RE FINALLY FEELING SOME RAGE.

YOU'D BETTER BE QUICK, OR IT'LL BE TOO LATE.
LOOK. ONLY VEGETA AND TRUNKS ARE HOLDING THEIR OWN.
GOKU'S LOST TOO MUCH ENERGY.

WOK
KKH

READ
THIS
WAY

GAAAH!!!

VUK
!!

HYAH
!!!!
THOK

ZUK

THIS IS RIDICULOUS!!
I CAN'T BE HAVING
THIS MUCH TROUBLE
AGAINST THESE
LITTLE SHRIMPS!!

THEY'RE ALL GOING TO DIE...!! IF I REALLY HAVE HIDDEN POWERS, I'VE GOT TO USE THEM...!!

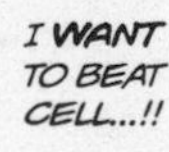

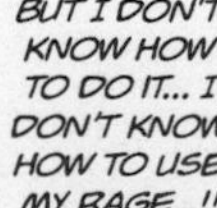

READ
THIS
WAY

YEESH...
WH-WHAT'S GOING ON...?!

WE'RE IN TROUBLE...
WE OUGHTTA GET OUT OF HERE...

W... WAIT...
YEEK ?!

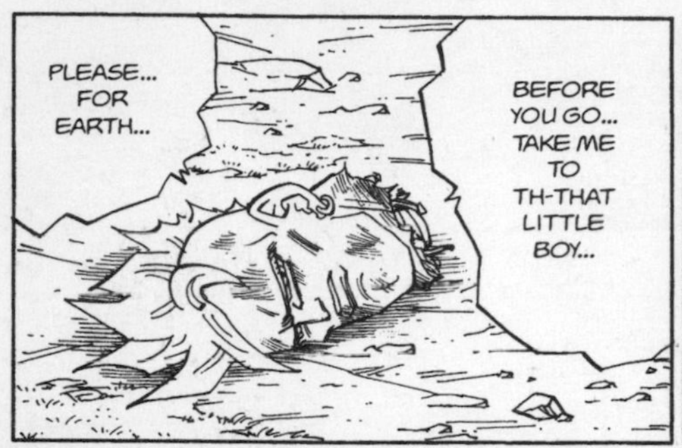
BEFORE YOU GO... TAKE ME TO TH-THAT LITTLE BOY...
PLEASE... FOR EARTH...

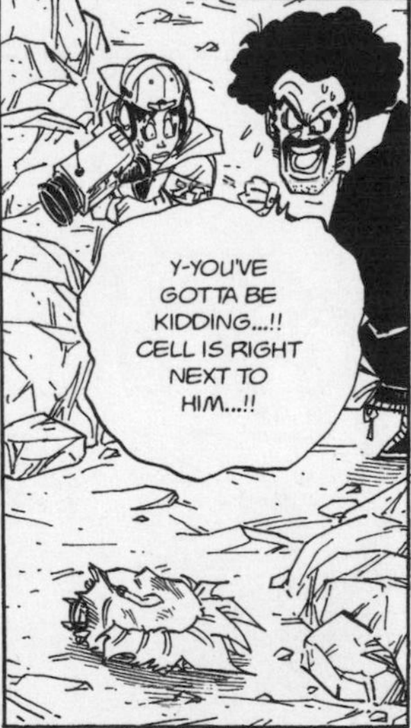
Y-YOU'VE GOTTA BE KIDDING...!! CELL IS RIGHT NEXT TO HIM...!!

DON'T YOU WANT TO HELP?
YOU'RE THE WORLD CHAMPION, AREN'T YOU...?

HERCULE IS A **HUMAN** CHAMPION! TH-THIS IS A BATTLE OF FREAKS!!

...

READ THIS WAY

ALL RIGHT!! I'LL DO IT!!

HERCULE, DON'T!! YOU'LL BE KILLED!!

SHUT UP!! ALL THESE NO-NAMES ARE OUT THERE FIGHTING!!
I'LL BE A LAUGHING STOCK IF I, THE CHAMPION, RUN AWAY!!

YOU JUST WANT ME TO TAKE YOU CLOSER, RIGHT...?
SNEAK
SNEAK
YEAH. THANKS.

ACTUALLY, I'M PRETTY SCARED...
JUST THROW ME WHEN YOU GET CLOSE ENOUGH.
OKAY! GREAT!

THOK
HIII!

READ
THIS
WAY

TOK
TOK

ZMP

P-
PLEASE
STOP...
I'M
BEGGING
YOU...

HEH HEH!
JUST A
LITTLE MORE
PERSUASION...

ALL RIGHT,
CELL
JUNIORS!!
ENOUGH
FOOLING
AROUND!!
YOU
CAN KILL
THEM
NOW IF
YOU
WANT
!!

!!

READ
THIS
WAY

TWK
TWK

YES... ALMOST THERE... !

DO IT!! KILL THEM !!!

H-HERE WE GO...!!
VNN

DOP
ROLLL
ROLLL

EH ?

TH-THE ANDROID...

SHOOT!! I THREW TOO HARD...!!

READ THIS WAY

S-SON GOHAN...
IT'S NOT A CRIME TO FIGHT FOR GOOD.
THERE ARE SOME WHO WILL NEVER LISTEN TO WORDS.

FEEL THE ANGER... SET YOUR PASSIONS FREE...
I KNOW HOW YOU FEEL... BUT YOU DON'T HAVE TO HOLD BACK.

GOOD ADVICE.
BUT I'M TRYING TO DO THIS MY WAY.

THE WILD ANIMALS AND THE FORESTS I LOVED... DON'T LET THEM BE DESTROYED...
PRO-TECT THEM FOR ME...

...

KNNCH

MIND YOUR OWN BUSINESS... RUST BUCKET.

WAAAAAAAAH!!!!!

HOOOSH

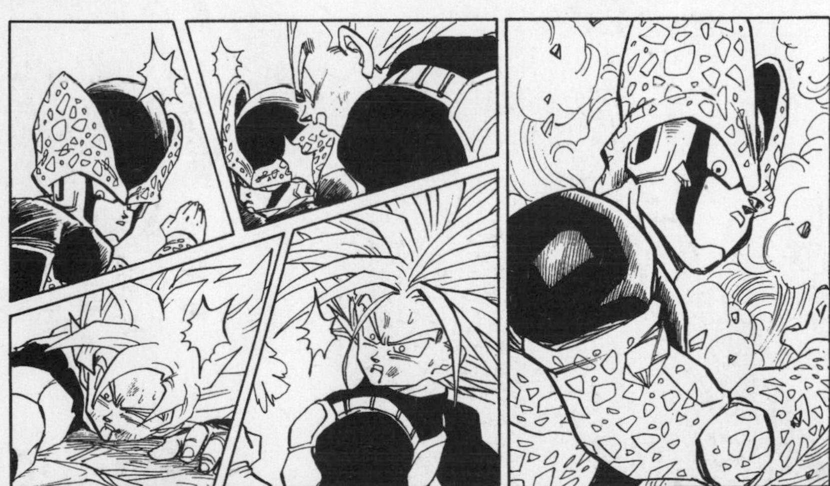

NEXT: Gohan Explodes!!

DBZ: 214 • Gohan Unleashed

VNNN

NOW YOU'RE IN FOR IT...

...ALL OF YOU.

ZK

ZK

...!!

BRRRT

BRRRT

READ THIS WAY

SO... YOU'VE FINALLY SHOWN YOUR TRUE FORM!! THIS... SHOULD BE INTERESTING...

SSW

HUH ?!

READ THIS WAY
Y-YOU TOOK THE SENZU... !!!
!!

HEE HEE...
HYAH !!!
BOOM

READ THIS WAY

ZOD

PWIK PWIK

HA...
I KNEW IT...

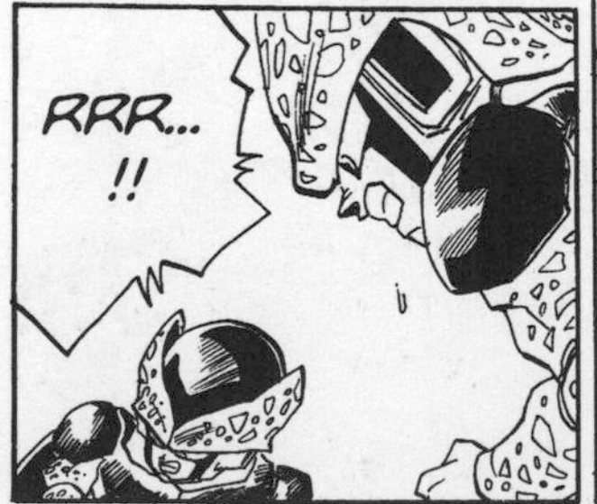
RRR...
!!

YE-
EE-
EE
!!!!

HYAAAA
!!!!

BOM

BOM

READ THIS WAY
ZZDDDD
BMF

READ THIS WAY

BLOPE

YEEK !!!
B-BMP

HHHHH

READ THIS WAY

DOOM

BLSH

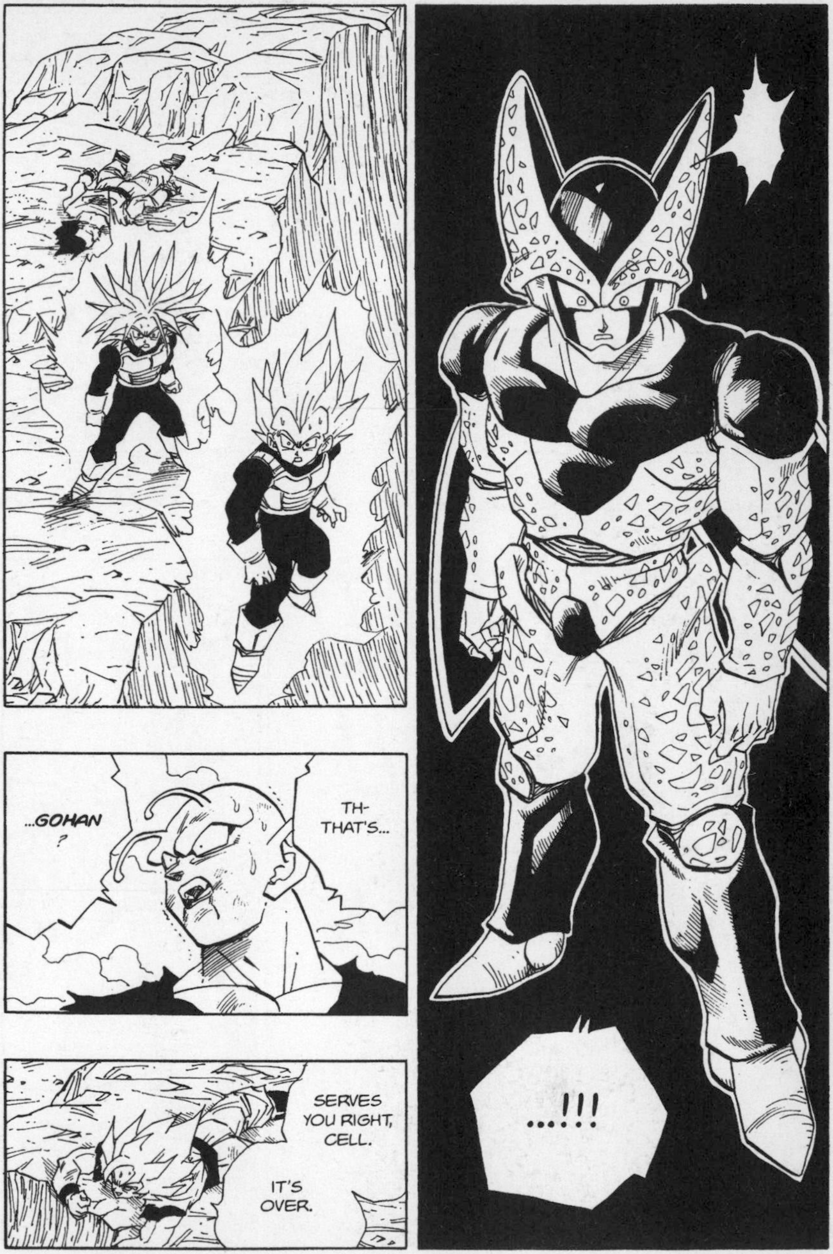

READ THIS WAY

...!!!

NEXT: Cell Gets Serious

TITLE PAGE GALLERY

These title pages were used when these chapters of **Dragon Ball Z** were originally published in Japan in 1993 in **Weekly Shonen Jump** magazine.

DRAGON BALL

とりやまあきら
鳥山明
BIRD STUDIO

DBZ:205
The Highest Level

ドラゴンボール

DRAGON BALL

ドラゴンボール

とりやまあきら

鳥山明

BIRD STUDIO

DBZ:206 • Ring Out

DRAGON BALL
ドラゴンボール
DBZ:208
Last Resort
とりやまあきら
鳥山明
BIRD STUDIO
TIME TO CHOOSE!!!

DRAGON BALL

ドラゴンボール

DBZ:209 The Successor

DRAGON BALL

ドラゴンボール

DBZ:212

#16's Secret Weapon

WHEN WE LOOK BACK, THOSE DAYS SEEM SO PEACEFUL... BUT THERE'S NO TIME TO LOOK BACK IN A FIGHT!

DRAGON BALL

BIRD STUDIO

ドラゴンボール

とりやまあきら 鳥山明

DBZ:213 • The Little Cells

DRAGON BALL

ドラゴンボール

DBZ:214

Gohan Unleashed

HERO, THY NAME IS GOHAN!

IN THE NEXT VOLUME...

Awakening to his true power, the once meek Gohan challenges Cell, the former strongest being alive! But even if he loses, Cell has a last desperate option–destroy the entire planet! Can the Saiyans and their allies save the world from being turned into a cinder? With the deaths of six billion people only seconds away, Goku and Gohan–father and son–must fight together to deal the final blow...

AVAILABLE NOW!

テニスの王子様
THE PRINCE OF TENNIS™

RATED
A
FOR
ALL AGES

VIZ media

SUBSCRIBE TODAY & BECOME A MEMBER OF THE SHONEN JUMP SUBSCRIBER CLUB...
You'll get:
*Access to Exclusive Online Content!
*50% Savings Off the Newsstand Price!
*Exclusive Premiums!
All this available ONLY to Subscribers!
SHONEN JUMP
THE WORLD'S MOST POPULAR MANGA
FILL OUT THE SUBSCRIPTION CARD ON THE OTHER SIDE, OR SUBSCRIBE ONLINE AT:
www.shonenjump.com